The Cracks Beneath Me

Idelis Llenas

To my family: You held my pain in your hearts and tended my inner garden until every withered part inside of me began to flourish in abundance again.

CONTENTS

TO YOU (YES YOU)

You have created webs out of your misfortunes. Proudly let
your fissures glow. Those in(visible) marks on your body–
they are part of who you are. Show them off. I dedicate this
to you and all that you've been through. Like you, I've been
through them too.

A NOTE

I have hurt in so many ways. Ranging from emotional leading to physical and, ultimately, sexual abuse. It is a tragedy that so many women suffer at the expense of their abusers. We are silenced by other people's doubts of our very own words.

I am here to tell you, that I learned to fall in love again. I learned to fall in love with life, fall in love with those who matter the most to me, and most importantly, fall in love with myself. He tried to erase my love from me until it left no trace behind. It has been an emotional roller coaster but still, my love was stronger than the turbulence.

I hope that my words help other survivors realize that they can prevail. Their cracks beneath them prove it.

DAWN'S EMBRACE

Dawn crept. It was a new day. She coddled me into her nurturing arms and advised me that everything would be okay. It was a new day. The sun was forgiving on my somber eyes as my body curled on her thighs. "Don't let your skin burn beyond recognition." I promised her I wouldn't. Dawn changed me. She bestowed upon me the opportunity for a second beginning. It was a new day.

It will be okay. It will be okay.

Cracks Beneath Me|

Barehanded,
I picked up pieces to shards
that weren't even mine.
I sliced cracks into my
skin of concrete
and bled blood that
wasn't even mine,
to appease someone
that didn't let me
be mine.

Pandora And Her Box|

You cautioned me of all the truth
opening you up would uncover.
I went along and tipped your
top wide open anyway.
I thought I'd find *hope* sprawled
across the bottom of your
embellished exterior.

Instead, I discovered lies decorated
with embroidered promises.
They may as well have been wearing
frilly ribbons; you hid them so well.

I warned you, you told me
but the damage had been done.

She Will Rebuild Again|

Her body is home.
She's spent a lifetime
building it; where will she go
if you damage the base of its existence?
She lived a life under a variety of shells—
you destroyed each and every one,
expecting her to run to you
for shelter at the midst of
stormy weather.

You Were Not Sorry...|

when you threatened to undress
the little I had on, so that you
could parade my naked
     body
          on
               the
                    crippled
                         streets.
When you sold me the story
of wanting to sell me for
five dollars or less
     because I
          wouldn't
               go
                  for
                      much.
You were not sorry. Even so,
forgiveness is not something I owe.

If It Makes You a Man|

If you can hit her,
you can also look
your mother in the
eyes and tell her
what you've done.

Survivor's Guilt|

Saving the rabbit
symbolized saving myself
and I wonder, after my
escape from your evil,
did you go back to the meadow
where I let her go?
Did you kill her
like you murdered
my soul?

I Haven't Died Yet|

If words permeated themselves on our skin
as we spoke them, you would be a
cemetery and I would be

                    a garden.

Unhealthy|

When you feel that you need to redact your thoughts, sucking them into a deep void like hitting backspace on a keyboard...

When you begin to feel allergic to their presence; a red and swollen throat, heaving lungs nearing corruption ...

When the space is vast and you have shrunken to nothing yet it still feels like you are occupying most of the empty space...

Leave.

What follows will only serve to contaminate you.

Undressed, In More Ways Than One|

I guess I should accept this as a part of me now. I used to be afraid to show my scathed skin; now, you can see ripples even through my clothes. They've become invisible. Life has an interesting sense of humor, you know. It'll spin you around and around in circles, your eyes adjust to the onset of vertigo, and you become immersed in the illusion that everyone is spinning just like you. Only when it comes to a sudden stop do you realize that those people were walking in pursuit: a destination. When your head finally stops spinning and your eyes finally regain focus like putting on glasses for the first time, you realize that you haven't got a place to go. The barrier between you and them is a bubble, a bubble that functions like a two-way mirror; you can see them but they can't see you. They were never spinning to begin with. The bubble abruptly pops, you heave the oxygen into your lungs, you toss your head back and up to the sky; people stare. They analyze you as if you were celestial art that somehow materialized from thin air. There's no going back, no hiding the wounds and bare broken flesh. Life has an interesting sense of humor because even as they bear witness to your nakedness, they still don't understand.

Seaweed|

My emotions intertwined themselves
with a slimy sticky sheen of doubt
until they obnoxiously
filled the ocean
in green.

The Way Our Minds Work|

Oddly enough,
I have faith that I'll trust again.
We are humans;
after all.
I hope, for your sake,
you will learn the vitality
of empathy,
as you hadn't learned
while you were on top of me–
as I begged for
your mercy.

It's Not Love, It's Abuse|

When someone takes it upon themselves to break the person that you created yourself to be, it isn't losing them that hurts you. It's the fact that it was so simple to tear down your foundation for the sake of their ego that stings. Destroying a person because of who they are is the equivalent of gratifying oneself with corrupted vanity; it satisfies their hunger for happiness transiently by slathering you like slime with their ill intentions.

They will pick you apart layer by layer just to say that they could. Then, they will profess their love to you by gifting you roses with thorns and making you hold them until blood trickles past the palms of your hands and down your forearms; they know you don't like clipped flowers because they die quickly. It is the principle in the meaning that they enjoy.

No matter how they may try to convince you, remember, *love is not supposed to make you bleed.*

His Version|

There is the kind of man,
who will try to take
management over you.

He will waltz in with a
smooth-like charm that you
won't resist.

He will want to skip
to the end of the race.

He will joke a little
too harshly.

He will play fight a little
too hard.

He will smile into the eyes of
folks that are closest to
you; shake hands, invite them to dinner.

Skip dinner. Tell them something came up.
An emergency. A nuisance.

She doesn't feel well.
A case of bad luck.

Her Version|

Being with him is a privilege.
I should be lucky, he says.
Let's spare your family
the agony.

They're tired of you.
He says.

They don't love you.
He says.

They won't save you.
He says.

Dinner's canceled.
Something came up.

Two fists and a cup.

I'm bleeding.
I'm falling.
I'm giving up.

I Should've Met You First|

Maybe, one day, you'll see
that the day I met you
my poetry grew its
own rhythm.

You Missed The Mark|

You scavenged for affection in
areas where affection didn't exist.
Between her thighs.
Below her hips.

Handyman|

She is not your toolbox. You don't get to
choose which of her pieces to use when
one of your damaged parts needs a repair.

Three Steps Back|

You accused me of living perfectly
at a point in time where
I was just trying to
mend the broken
        parts of me.

Envious hearts don't know—
perfection is at a distance
that we can't reach.

Envious hearts don't know—
imperfection has a charm
that can cost a leg and arm.

You accused me of living perfectly
when I'd just solved the mystery
of living inside a body
riddled with
        uncertainties.

I Can't Forgive And I Can't Forget|

Water droplets slide down my body;
the steam encloses itself around me.
I rest my left forearm on my knee
and my forehead on my wrist.

Then I think,
again,
again,
and again.

Mainly about how I got to the brink
of whatever this is and how I let him
tarnish my brown skin.

Domino Effect|

You laid me like pieces—
one after the other,
all in one line.

With a brush of a finger
you toppled me over
once, my love,
you could not find.

Imprisoned By Questions|

Everything is so bright outside
and yet, I feel so gray.
The sun beamed on my tattered clothes,
your jeans hung low on my hips,
my sneakers welded themselves
in the mud beneath me.
Blood had started to crust on my lips
and on the cut on my brow.
Do you remember the darkness?
It is all that I recalled;
icy, devilish, crystal blue eyes
glaring past my human flesh
in your one man boiling brawl.
Did you feel like a man?
When your palms met the skin
you once claimed was *oh so soft.*
Did you feel like a man
when you stripped me of my humanity?
Did you feel anything at all?

Irony Begins With I|

He puffed on cigarettes as if he could absorb life out of the tobacco. He depended on Marlboro to revive the dead parts of him; the charred ashes of whatever his brain was battling that day.

She didn't judge him. Who was she to, anyhow? On most days, he leaned his hand out of the car window and balanced the cigarette between his forefinger and his middle; she used to admire the beauty in all that tragedy. That is, until the day he tried to see if there was any life he could take from her.

She no longer sees the beauty in self-destruction, no matter how vague.

Sinners In Denial|

We were both troubled
but not in the same ways;
that's what drew us to
one another, wasn't it?

The Jolly Cow |

You wiped the upper tip
of your ice cream cone
on my soft pointed nose
and, for the first time,
neither of us felt so alone.

I guess that's what we craved,
a platonic paired camaraderie,
a head bopping car session
with the music bumped up
and someone like you

and someone like me.
It reminded us both
that none of us were built
to be completely vertically.
The day tasted like vanilla ice cream.

God, I'd thought,
how much I wanted this on my lips;
two diametrically opposed energies,
our tales of misadventure lost
in our strawberry creamed kiss.

False Oath|

I didn't say 'I love you'
for reasons you didn't understand.
It would have been like
giving a fourth of my heart
and swearing an oath
with my left hand.

Overdose|

Simply, you were
too much for my
mind, body, soul.

I almost died rid-
ding your toxic
waste from my

system– left to
battle the effects
of my mistakes.

I Hope That They Believe Me|

I hope that they believe me when I say that if they were to go back to where he confined me, they could probably still smell my fear on his sheets dating back seven months from this date. I hope that they believe me when I say that I cried and screamed no– despite the fight I put up, he chose to see past the stop sign on my face, continuing to cut through all my red lights. I hope that they believe me when I say he kept the lights off, as to not see my skin swelling as a product of his inadmissible rage.

I hope that they believe me when I say I needed to be ready. I hope that they believe me once I tell my story.

Elastic Heart|

You wrapped me around with my elastic heart
until my small chest began to heave.
When things started to fall apart,
you refused to let me leave.

I traveled through your vessels;
remembered the outline of your veins.
Emanated a love that stretched for miles
and left the imprint on your brain.

Promises Of Blue|

Was it true?
Was it true when you promised
        everything would be okay?
You promised me blue,
instead I see gray.
        How come you're not here today?
I painted my walls last night–
if broken were a color, that's what
        I would have slathered them in.
But instead, I chose blue,
the one color that reminds me of you.
        Remember our walks in the garden?
You used to pick out the best daffodil,
place it behind my ear and remind me
        that they symbolized hope.
The daffodil died that evening,
taking me with her
        and leaving behind
your promises of
blue.

Mishap|

As the passage of time
rusted the nails a light tint
of orange-brown, the
plywood began to
reject each
      i n d i v i d u a l l y.

They clinked onto the
floor, day by day, one by one.
A single one remained
before her structure
collapsed and she
could no longer
      h i d e.

Hotel Hell|

My mind became a prison that I couldn't escape– it felt as though I was forced to repeat the same routine every day. That's what became of me because of you; four walls, the intruding feeling of confinement, being completely unable to escape thoughts of what you had done. Ultimately, I became the prison and the prisoner. It is ironic that I spent what felt like eternity trying to break free from your restraints but, somehow, I still confine myself in your chains.

Lost Poems|

She bled stories through her fingers,
as they reaped merciless cries,
"*save me,*

     save me,

save me."
Hoping, for once, that they would be
heard.

A Metaphor|

There is so much hunger inside of me, a
lavish exquisite hunger that will not settle
for less than a three-course meal.

I have searched across the border for the
utmost delicacies to silence my
unsolicited craving but all that seems to
be left for me are crumbs.

It Was Rape|

You touched me in all the ways
I didn't want you to–
in all of the places
I didn't want you to
and without my permission.

Mother|

There is not a single word to describe
all the strength you've planted inside of me
by watering me with words of wisdom
       when I was just a fragile seed.

"A resentful heart is too heavy to harbor,
burdens such as those should be set free."
Instead, you gifted me armor,
       "the least of your worries are bloody
knees."

Within my roots you carved so deeply
phrases that will never fade,
"A woman can be just as good a warrior–
       best of all– she doesn't need a blade."

More Than Average|

If only I had known,
that my skin isn't just skin
and my bones aren't just bones.
My body is more than casual entertainment.

The damage you fermented onto every aspect of me
could have possibly been prevented.
If I had loved myself a bit more.
If only I had known before.

Breaking And Entering|

Breaking into my sanctuary,
rummaging through the spiders
hidden in the crevices of my attic
with an endearing curiosity that only
you could understand.

Entering my most prized possession,
tenaciously grasping it in your fists;
a peasant discovering a fortune.
You used them to bandage your actions—
initially forgetting what they meant to me.

Choose Your Path|

His departure is not your undoing–
it is your rebirth, your manifestation.
It is the recreation of your eternal growth.
He may have lent you the fuel
       but you were always in the driver's seat.

Her Story|

What if tomorrow I don't come back? What if I turn away and cease to be, to you? What if I, for once, choose our path and it turns out to be the end?

She had an impressive knack for disappearing and this time was no exception. She had poured herself into him until he couldn't have enough of her. She became his habit, his air, and now that he was whole, she needed to find her own way, carve her own path, seal her own fate. This wasn't it. Glorifying a life of healing damaged people wasn't it.

So, she disappeared.

She healed, she disappeared, and now she was reaching the end of her selfless journey. She made a profession out of mending people with imprints in their lives that she often longed for it. She longed for a life of totality even more. Their pieces had become a part of her and now she was sealed with a substance stronger than adhesive.

She didn't long for a half.

She craved a complemented counterpart.

Invasion|

There wasn't much left
by the time you finished

but you insisted on looking
for something that
was not there.

Had I remained,
you would have dug
into places unknown to me.
                    This is what pervades my
thoughts.

Preventive Measures|

I bound my legs together
with an imaginary rope
so that no man can
try to forcibly tear
my legs open
again.

It Wasn't My Time|

You didn't think it would be a crime
to incinerate a rose for heat,
leaving its debris wandering
       aimlessly.

Vultures don't shed tears
when attacking their enemy.
You must have forgotten that
       when you went for me.

You cried at my burial
and watered my seeds;
I flourished again, thanks
       to your trying greed.

Redwood|

Some say, *all great writers*
have witnessed hell
to some degree.

Well, I say, you can't
reach your roots
if there is no tree.

The wise
don't make the wise
without a bit of history.

NOON'S GIFT

Noon had always been so generous to me. He
knew I loathed cold weather and gifted me you
right before my worst winter. I have experienced
the highs and I have experienced the lows but I am
no longer reluctant to conquer blizzards.

We can fight our storms. We can fight them
together.

Tidal Waves|

You washed over me
all of a sudden, one day.

No matter how hard I tried
I couldn't push you away.

You enveloped yourself
around my body–

I should have been afraid
of such an inviting tidal wave.

Only the strongest hearts
grow a love so brave.

Common Courtesy|

All I ask of you is to please be kind to my body before divulging yourself into me. It's taken enough beatings already. I'm not ashamed of my phantom bruises because they signify that I survived. However, people think it's clever to probe the same spot until something surfaces and claim it was accidental. *I'm sorry sweetie, I didn't mean it,* they'd say. Then, proceed to handle me as if I were a monthly rental. They will look me over, scrutinize me, take note of the markings, and then act surprised that they're there. I'm not some cheap motel cinema movie that you watch when your girl walks out the door with declarations of never coming back. I'm what makes the content, baby. I am the writer, the director, the producer; I am so much more than the falsehood you've created in your mind. I am the reality behind the fabrication and frankly, I've put too much effort into this. So much so that I'd rather be stamped with the word arrogant than to let one more person damage it. Sorry to ruin your movie but please be kind to my body.

Eternal|

You know your heart is filled
with all that has value;
trickles of passion
detailing who
and what
        you walk the ground for.
But honey, there is still
room for more love.
Your heart is
infinite
        but only for the right things.

Only for the right moments.
Only for the right people.

Compass|

We crossed paths.
Neither one with open eyes.
Subsequently, we found ourselves.
Enticed by our ethereal lives.

Love At First Sight|

A sudden pang momentarily disoriented me—
it was as if the earth stopped rotating.

Nothing else mattered.
Everything froze under a thin sheet of ice.

Time was no longer relevant,
our tasks momentarily faded in front of our eyes.

We glanced at each other for a second too long.
You spoke to me before we exchanged words.

This is what it felt like;
the calm.

Formality|

You analyzed the periphery of my hips—
      letting your mouth study
the intricacies of aged wine;
      brushed your fingers on my lips,
letting drunken words fill the space between us.
      "How much of me would I have to give
in order to get a taste of this?"
      "Not a finger, not a leg, not a dollar, not a cent—
a girl like me is worth more than half a glass.
      A girl like me is priceless."

Self-Love Before His Love|

I fooled myself into believing that
if I could mold into what
you wanted, you would
realize I was there
all along.

It took some time before I learned–
you didn't know what you wanted;
you did not get to me
       before you were already gone.

A Short Distance To Forgiveness|

I write poetry about you
to remind myself that
people are cut from
an all too familiar cloth
but distinguish their blankets
through different lenses.
Like a colorblind man
who'd never see the color
of the sunset through
the hues of the conventional norm;
two sides of the same coin,
two ends of the same storm.

With Benefits|

We weren't much, if anything at all. There was no love story to tell; no roses, no dates, no surprise proclamations of love. It was just us. We were two people. We were two lonely people like other lonely people in the world. We used each other to temporarily numb what was missing in our lives when the moment called for it. We were human. Could we be blamed? If I could admit something to you, I'd say,

'It was terrifying. Anything, any single thing, could have ruptured our unspoken pact to hold each other when there was no one else to hold. Usually, for me, there was no one else worth holding. It was beyond loneliness for me. It was you. It always has been. This could have been enough to make you stray, so silent I remained."

Stay|

I have never been one to beg; though,
it is not difficult to admit that
my fibers have fallen
victim to you.

Don't Let Go|

I was taught from young
to be gentle.

Not in the way I touch
but in the way I
empathize.

The significance of an embrace
was a stamped 'void' sign
into my existence,
until the day
       you wrapped your arms around me.

Fortress|

If he ever tries to use
you as an aged mat,
let him know that
he is no longer
welcome.

Treat Her With Value|

Is it the glowing bronze of her complexion
that causes you to misperceive her
as an item meant to be disposed?

She may be dense like burning ember
but her skin is made of gold.

Montage|

Moments of you flip constantly
like an old movie screen
in my mind.

And although we haven't
shared much of our time
together, I've learned to

memorize the structure
of your jawline
when you smile.

And although we are
separated for more than
just a mile,

I can still feel how you lightly
brushed my thigh, even you
knew it somehow felt right.

And although these memories
of we are exclusive to me,
flashes of you

are printed like
invisible ink
on paper,

flickers that only I can see.

10:30PM|

Your lips were like honey;
warm, forgiving, pure.
How simple it was—
losing myself in your kisses.
It almost gave me a
sliver of faith. That perhaps,
one day I'd be more than
a nighttime muse
to you.

My Confession|

I find comfort in you
because you are
a calm sea—
so so sweet.

It feels like I found home.
I could never
tell you
          but how I wish that you would know.

Father|

You taught me that sugar is sweet
but that sometimes life tends to feed you salt.
You taught me that lemons are tasty
with two ice cubes, water, and a cup.
You taught me that I would have to make it
and every so often, I won't have the
components that are required.
You taught me that I would not have to long for,
I could attain what I desired.
You taught me that a man's two good uses are
his hands and, sometimes, maybe his brain.
You taught me that it truly matters
how the man that claims to love me
wakes up and says my name.
You taught me that gentleness is the
minimum prerequisite of what it means to care.
You taught me that a man should treat me well
by the way that you have been there.
You taught me that the man I marry
should not come short to all that you have
sacrificed and all that you have done.
You taught me that a man who truly devotes his
time to me–after him– I should never have to run.

Create|

Your temples will pulse;
throbbing, aching pain.
Create.
It will hurt,
it is not meant to be easy.
Create.
This is who you are.
Create.
Sacrifice will owe you a favor.

Broken Wings|

People have often told me,
there are certain things in life
that you just never forget
once you learn them.

Riding a bike, knitting,
driving a car, swimming.
You damaged my wings,
yet I managed to soar–
            I had never learned to fly before.

Evaporative Quality|

Knowing you was the equivalent
to being wrapped in mist.
Present enough to be felt,
constantly dissipating,
never in pursuit
to solidify–
       yet you were there.

Sequences|

I push. You pull. You push. I pull.
Either way, we find ourselves
immersed in each other;
the city has always
offered its silence.

We don't know how we got there,
we don't try and ask.
It is our secret,
this little secret.

It isn't much. But it's a start.

The Balloon Effect|

I want to love you in a way that
swells your chest and
expands your mind.
        I want to love you immeasurably.

Larger Than Life|

In your pursuit to see him as the world,
you neglected to look into his pupils.
You could've seen that every time
his eyes aimed in your direction
      the universe was in their reflection.

Falling|

An anchor is strapped to my ankle,
I am sinking into an abyss.
Lifeboats; nowhere to be found—
engulfed in deep sea bliss.

If tonight I stop submerging,
I would like to tell you this…
mornings are only mornings
when awoken by your kiss.

Uncomfortable Comfort Zone|

I've noticed that when I'm with you
words seem to clog themselves
at the bottom of my
esophagus.

They assemble a nest for each other,
each anxious to evolve into
something better but
waiting
      until it is their time to do so.

Acrobat|

Meticulously, I placed one foot
on the tightrope; it threatened to
curve beyond its full capacity—
a taunting façade to derail me
from reaching your end.

Love is the strangest of all.
In my unwavering commitment,
I did without a harness but
at my arrival
          I relied on your hands to catch my fall.

Our Plot|

I don't want to be the main theme of your life. Hold your subjects dearly because I could never imagine taking that away from you. If possible, I want to water your plot with meaning. Dazzle it with adventure and spontaneity. Let me decorate it when all else is stale. We'd share morals and lessons like we share kisses but I would never want to reign over those dearest to you. I would never want to pry away what matters. I am not asking to be your main theme but a small part, whichever fits the hour, would be sufficient.

Almost Fairytale|

From one moment to the next,
our faces had met until
his nose grazed
                mine.

He confidently brushed his lips;
no force could stand to stop us.
Lonely souls fighting, fighting
                against time.

Our lust filled hands searched
over seemingly endless skin.
Looking for and hoping to find
                an almost happy end.

Every Part Of You Is Useful|

Your tears have produced oceans,
brought crops to fruition,
they have nurtured.

They yield viability.
Never let yourself
be afraid to feel.

Waiting Game|

The leaves have run dry.
Seasons have shifted past me.
You have yet to call.

Come Home Soon|

Warmth is knowing that I can hold you
without worry of another
cold and desolate
winter.

Clichés|

I wanted you to be
the one who chased me
down Grand Central station
for one last and final goodbye caress.

I wanted you to be
the one I bumped into
while I fumbled inside of my bag—
our words blending into apologies.

I wanted you to be
the one to show me stars
even though you never studied
ecosystems or the basic principle of astrology.

I wanted you to be
the one.

Side Effects|

You were a prescription,
I didn't know how much
I needed you in my system.
Somehow you alleviated all my
                    inner symptoms.

I took you in so easily;
pills have never been
hard for me to swallow.
I needed you in my system knowing
                    you could be gone
tomorrow.

The Edge|

I lived for you.
Knowing that I might enter
a place that I
have never known.

I lived for you.
My vessels crooned
when my organs
faltered.

They knew.
They knew that
I lived for you.

Never mind, Neverland|

I used to imagine that I would,
one day, wake up to the vibration
        of your warm words on my cheeks.
Hoping, hoping, hoping
that your body would, in due time,
manifest
        next to mine.
Like warm cookies on Christmas–
a delicacy with hidden potential to
        nourish my spirit.
You would awaken the child in me;
liberated, creative, and sweet.
        But you never showed,
and so, I was forced to grow.

Cheers to Hoping|

It was like a congested longing,
filling the brim until she could
no longer breath.

Only he could empty out the blocked
unspoken thoughts of her
devoted affections.

Magnets|

There is a slight difference between lust and love. Lust wasn't the one that texted me at 5pm to see how I was doing.

The Medusa Effect|

The air I breathe is liquid cement,
molding itself inside of my lungs
each day that passes by where,
        to you, nothing I have meant.

My heart keeps anticipating that
tomorrow I will hold some meaning
in the inner depths of your heart before
        I'm made of nothing but stone.

You Were Never Mine|

No matter how hard I attempted to
grip the sand in the palms of my hands,
the grains slipped right through my fingers.
Unfortunately, I made the same mistake with
you.

Attempted Reminder|

He will only want you
when it conveniences him.
Don't let yourself confuse it for more.
If it is 1am on a Friday,
don't show up at his door.
You are too beautiful to open your thighs
for someone who will dig two fingers
inside of you as if he's lost
something rare yet will
refuse to look at
you in the eyes.

Rarity|

Tell him to stop searching
for jewels in your
sacred spaces.

If he couldn't spot that
you are the jewel, when
he first ran into you, then
even he knows that he
doesn't deserve someone
as precious as you.

Your Memory Of Me|

Amidst the straying crowd,
your face, I'd like to see.
Within the hazy fog
is where I'd like to meet.

When I've succumbed to
a plethora of unrequited emotions,
I'll have no choice but to leave
with hazy memories of you
        as my one and final token.

Companionship|

Women laughing,
children flying in the arms
of their fathers,
couples peck
rosebud cheeks,
pelicans call to their
mates,
a yellow panorama
fading into orange.
And I always,
on the outside
looking in.

In Another Life|

One night, you will tell me,
Goodbye. So it will be.
The end of our era
in each other's
company.

A Message From The Stars|

"Above all, I hope you can bask
in the greatness that you are.
I assure you, I'm okay. We
were not written in the
stars. All that I ask
is that you know
the twinkle that
you see is from
me."

Second Chances |

Maybe tomorrow
       is meant to come
       to undo all that
       we have done.
Maybe yesterday
       was meant to pass
       so we can do
       better than the last.
And if today
       we lose our way,
       take solace in
       the chance to begin
again.

Persistence|

I will write until I have
nothing else to say, no more
                    emotions to feel.
I will write until the end of my days
—at the beginning of my sorrows—
I will write now, later and
                    tomorrow.

Keep Your Wilted Flowers|

Have you stopped to think that maybe the ground splits beneath you so that you could see how undervalued the roots can be? So often, we strip beauty from its surface, without as much of a second thought as to what we may be damaging on the inside. Our roots may tangle but they are what keep us alive.

We Aren't Ours|

It wasn't lost on me that I was not your 'kind' of woman, you had made that abundantly clear. What I wish you had known at the time, what I wish I could have explained to you is that, I was not trying to be your kind of woman. I was trying to be my kind of woman. I was working to be the best version of myself and because you couldn't understand that, you were not my 'kind' of man.

Opposites Attract|

We weren't the best dancers but I enjoyed dancing with you. I would put the stereo on, the song wouldn't make sense; it didn't fit our description. I twirled, letting the patterned tempo pulse through my lungs. You would join in, grab my hand, and we would dance until the dawn. We didn't take the same steps but the beat we had, it was ours.

Honesty|

How many women have you
let down with those
fragile, fragile words
coated in nectar
and juvenility?
Please, tell me. I want to learn
how to hurt the way
that you meant me to.

Court Jester |

What a shame
that foolish hearts
tend to pleasure themselves
with heartache games.

Didn't you know?
You will never win
a game that was not
ever meant to be played.

Caring|

Every time I say I don't
I do a little more.

When the signs tell me to let go
I hold a tad bit tighter.

It makes my midnights darker
and my middays not much brighter.

Safety Net|

"Maybe you don't know,
though I have chosen
not to sink,
> *it has never taken two to swim."*

He said I would eventually
obliterate myself into nothing,
without the imagined comfort of his presence
to navigate me across the tough currents of life.

"I have been swallowed in darkness
repeatedly. It is an insult
to assume that I would
need another to help me
> *stay afloat."*

Strawberries|

He was into the kind of women
that smelled like strawberry and sin.
She could have tried to be like them;
fragranced herself in vodka and gin,
hiding the scent with innocence.
She did not choose to blend in.
He, instead, chose them.

Naïve|

As we ate, you had offered me a
piece of your steak... I hesitated
because I'd just began my
transition into vegetarianism.

I took a bite despite my conscious.

When you rejected me at night fall,
I learned never to exchange
peace of mind for
acceptance.

My Turn|

Perhaps, I can't provide
the circumference of
life that you seek.
Perhaps, I can't fill a
book with poetry of
your reveries.
Perhaps, you have decided
that I do not suffice
enough for we.
Still today, today, I will be
good enough
for me.

Yin and Yang|

The day spoke to her and said,
*"he is not what you need. Your
tired feet, they walk on their own."*

The night responded,
*"a journey traveled alone
is one less story told."*

Open Doors|

I decided to let you go
–not because I'm bitter–
from the outside,
it may seem so.

No.

I made a pact of many
to include myself in
my hopes, dreams.
Of many,
　　　　it is a pact I intend to keep.

War Cry|

She forgave in metaphors.
Her battlefield consisted of commas,
continuations, semicolons, interferences
and periods to mark the end of the war brewing
(inside of her).

She wanted to save the world in similes.
They would reach as high as towering skyscrapers.
They would defy the meaning of gravity; floating into
ears of those who deeply believed in conquering morally
(lived victories).

She overcame through the triumph of ink.
Letting the wreckage of combat seep through her hands.
Fumbling through the masses of long gone poems,
consolation brewed beneath her as she witnessed births
(of unspoken war cries).

I Will Sing My Sadness|

Once the tales pour out of my mouth
like a family of cocoons ready to emerge,
let me be seen, not as my cracked shell
but as a butterfly– designed by the
patterns of her life on the surface
                            of her wings.

Our Lost Song|

Conclusively, we
have no need for a love
vinyl to spin our scratched record.

Your New Start|

I'll sing to you a song of giving
expecting nothing in return.
I will wish you happiness,
fortune; all that you deserve.

You will slip right through my fingers
though–for you–my heart will yearn
and when you find a worthy figure,
her heart, I hope you earn.

But You Deserve It|

I will remember the nights that
I went to sleep at 3am trying
to decipher the perfect
words to describe
how you make
me feel in a
stanza.

You are
like an image
in a precious locket
that I am hesitant to
give to someone that you
may consider more beautiful,
more intelligent, more special, than I.

We Could Have Been|

"So just like that, you're moving out of town? Was this your way of saying a final goodbye?"

I had been sitting with my legs crossed, our blanket wrapped around my bare shoulders, my collarbones on full display. Goosebumps began to form on the visible parts of my skin.

"It was my final chance to show you that how I feel won't ever go away," I responded, letting the sheets slip down to the small of my back, exposing me bare. *"No matter where either of us are, our adventures were significant to me."*

I unfolded my legs and let my feet touch the cool floor tiles. The springs of the mattress pinged as I stood up and walked over to the other end of our hotel room. My back turned toward you, I could sense your stare trying to pull me– I managed to detach, grabbing the tail end of my shirt; pulling it over, one arm hole in, and then the other. I hadn't finished pulling the shirt on when I saw your figure manifest in front of me out of the shadows. You stood two feet away; your shoulders were broad and balanced to complement your stocky torso but when you drew me in it was like being stroked by a million different feathers.

"I'm sorry," you said, in a hushed tone out of the bleakness of our last embrace. *"I'm sorry that it took me this long to realize it."*

I pulled away gently, *"realize what?"*

"That I took your presence for granted and it's not fair to make you stay."

Silicone Fantasies|

Once, I persuaded myself
that we were bound by a string
but I lost sight of it;
mesmerized by the water,
down by the stream.

I waited 434 days
to see what patience would bring...
it took its time,
leaving me in a crowded city
filled with loneliness and torn up things.

Somewhere in between,
I let the current take me
into its arms.
It reclaimed its string of fate
and left me with my silicone fantasies.

Your Favorite Season|

Maybe I'm an autumn woman;
I am enough to suffice for the moment.
Impermanent.
Until the frostbites of winter weaken your bones
and make you crumble into yourself.
I am short and to the point; coming at
just the right time, at just the right moment.
Going when you've had your round.
I am the breeze that cools your spine
after a long summer; I make the hairs
on your arms stand instantaneously.
Maybe I'm an autumn woman
to a man who only wants the
comfort of summer air.

Birthright|

*"You change your hair as often as
you change your underwear,
it's like you're aching to be
a different woman."*

I've spent almost an entire life trying to
portray the perfect lady;
I forgot how to misbehave.
What can anyone say if
I'm not the same woman
from yesterday?

Teach Empathy Instead|

We are taught to be so afraid of silence;
sometimes, we forget that within the
      silence are the answers we search for.

We are taught to be so afraid to speak;
sometimes, we would rather listen
      to anything and anyone but the truth.

We are taught to be so afraid of ourselves;
sometimes, we wish to be someone else,
      forgetting that others are strapped

with a weight
    too
        heavy
           to
              carry.

It Gets Better, Kid|

Many always caution
that your present worries
will cease to matter a year from now.

They tell you to make a home for your burdens
inside a pair of boots that barely fit,
simultaneously, pulling the straps
with a too tight grip.

It's been a year; the boots
have worn themselves beyond
recognition– I am still here,
            unable to rid my mind of you.

A Minute Too Late|

Hi, how are you? How have you been?
It's been so long, I had often
wondered where you went.
I know you haven't asked
—maybe I shouldn't tell you—
I met a man in a café down
by the avenue, near the hotel,
where you and I used to stay.
We listened to jazz under a lamppost
when the moonlight was at its peak.
We shared secrets and wishes,
things we never dared to speak.
I cried on his shoulder,
do you know what he said?

"A man will only learn once he is out of your head."

I Will Park My Heart Elsewhere|

The pitter patters feel like the
ticket meter about to go off.
We've run out of time;
there was a limit on us
and a consequence for
surpassing the deadline.

Confession|

If you were to glimpse closely,
below the veins on my wrists,
you would see my past written
in modern hieroglyphics.

They masquerade as faded blemishes
that have decided to check in
the moment I met blade to skin,
intentionally forgetting their baggage,
         although I have rid my head of mine.

Acceptance|

The biggest lesson I have learned in this lifetime
is how to coexist with a body I didn't choose,
under unchangeable circumstances
and how to live remorselessly
despite it.

Indefinite |

We harmonized like a musician and her instrument;
I held the strings, you, the foundation.

Our composition may have crumbled
but our music never stopped.

Grownups|

I dreamt a dream of coffee and cream;
sun-kissed skin,
a sky with stars
and me and him.

I dreamt a dream, a silly child's dream;
a wedding on the beach,
the sand on our feet
and me and him.

I dreamt a dream with a white picket fence;
hot chocolate winters,
summers of lavender incense
and me and him.

I dreamt a dream of you and me;
arm in arm, heart to heart,
chest to chest,
too bad I haven't found you yet.

Lovestruck|

Serpents are elegant
but they are venomous,
they will slither into your life
with poise and sly determination.

Though her every move was gentle
       her love bites left you in a trance.

Finish Line|

Fire rips through my shins
as my feet pound the pavement.
A mass blur of structures and bodies
blend together to form a mesh of colors.

This, this racing heart, racing feet, racing life;
it was easier than slowing down to their speed.
Stopping meant having a vivid view,
it meant confronting my potential
                            to be happy.

Finale|

"After all this time, why do you still try?"

He had always looked as if he'd been chiseled from marble, buoyantly strong yet delicate as the sculptor's hands. Now, his slouched torso defeated him into childlike resignation.

The ferocity I lacked from all those I loved before him grew from my toes to my crown as I gazed intently into his ocean eyes and replied, *"Does the sun give up when the moon needs to rest?"*

DUSK'S HOMAGE

Dusk paid tribute to all the wreckage that leaked
from beneath me. She told me to remember.
Remember these stories. Not only for myself but
for everyone else. Speak them into the wind and
hope that they whistle into the ears of those who
need reassurance. 'You have gone through pain,
yes, but so have millions of others. Volunteer
your mouth and they will volunteer their
attention.'

My ode to you: A fresh horizon for us.

Me Too|

You do not owe anyone strength, so, I will not tell you to be strong. I will not advise you to hold against your tears– vacuuming them in like they are disposable and insignificant. You demonstrated your ferociousness through your mere survival. They don't know that as he taunted you with guilty fingers, it took all your power not to stoop to his inhumanity. That, my dear, is strength. Let your eyes moisten because though you have been vulnerable, your spine has stretched higher than it has ever been and you are present and your chest still thumps and that is strength.

Silver Lining|

It is a natural reaction for us
to avoid lightning when
it strikes.

If we look from a distance,
we see that it's only
doing its job.

Feeding the grass,
brightening it;
nitrogen into nitrates.

Like grass,
our lightning
is only a silver lining.

Civilized Uproar|

Your presence has the power to silence cities,
don't be afraid to stop earthquakes with your
words.

Phoenix |

Sometimes, all that matters are the simple things: the low humming of the wind as you sit on the warm bench by the water with thoughts in a vacant mind to accompany you. Never mind the guy who kindly rejected you because he was not 'that' into you; life is not gray, so you will forget him– at least for this moment.

Then, comes the revival of the wilting flower: literally and figuratively. Spring had sprung a pink June morning, the dew of rain left from yesterday had begun to clear away, leaving its trails behind with no remorse. Yes, she took her time arriving, but God, are you ever so grateful that she finally showed. Mother Nature served as did you– the devilish winter took its time, however, we ascended anew.

It was like, seeing the sun shine for the first time but being able to consciously process the value in its significance. It was as if I was being rebirthed into adulthood. The air sat fresh and light, the architecture of even the dullest buildings were of magnificence; standing grotesquely proud of their dimness. June was my Spring and she reflected it back to me so I would understand clearly; I was an infant in a woman's body. *"Learn what it means to live again,"* Spring said. I interconnected my fragility with my attained knowledge and removed the veil that hooded my tired eyes for so long. I was born again.

Nirvana|

She found peace in her craft; divulged in it,
memorized its bumps and ridges, and fell in love
with the texture. She didn't need to look anymore.
It seeped through her pores with nuclear
magnitude. There was no question, it was there to
stay– not in bits and pieces but in its entirety.
Stanzas. Lines. Verses. With that, she had no
reason to ever want again.

A Poet's Relations|

"I don't often get the chance to talk to someone like you."

I tilted my head up at him inquisitively, *"what do you mean, 'someone like me?'"*

"You know, someone who writes. Someone who isn't an open book but spills her questions and answers in ink. Someone who isn't afraid to put herself out there on paper and analyze at large. I can talk to you and feel like it means something more than what's here and now. It makes me appreciate it, it makes me appreciate you. It's this that makes me want to live a life worth documenting."

Afraid To Break|

"You were always so good at being alone. I didn't want to be the one to ruin that."

Your voice had only been a slight whisper–unknowingly, I peeled off a side of you that you hadn't meant to show. It never occurred to me that my doubts grew like mold in your life. I watched you twiddle your thumbs with forgiving eyes. You were soft, I was firm– unbreakable and willing to prove it. In that moment, my beliefs seemed to dissipate abruptly.

"I never wanted to be alone. I was afraid you'd find out that I'm made of glass."

Puzzle |

Blossom under the pressure
of those that look at you
under a wondering microscope.

You are meant to be a wanderer.
They will try to solve you
without all the pieces.

But you don't owe it to
anybody to hand them
your missing elements

if they were the ones
that misplaced them.

Aged Liked Wine|

I carried myself not in the
elegance of my body but
in the eloquence of my mind.

I lost many potential lovers.
I didn't exemplify the external extravagance
that the men I have often come across searched for.

I wore elegance not in my clothes.
It, instead, formulated itself in thoughts and words.
Though, it never seemed to suffice the minds of men.

I spent years trying to mold myself to be
the object of all their desires, forgetting that
I am fated to inspire.

A Journey Higher Than Us|

Her mission became to spread her tales.
She wanted to nourish the planet
so that it would speak her
phrases among the
            surrounding galaxies.

She fought so that her words
could one day become so strong
that anyone who looked at her could see them
            engraved in her aura.

Once And For All|

I do not want to speak for anyone.
I want my sentences to be
the element of courage
for those who are
too afraid to.

I do not want to form your opinion.
I want my experiences to
encourage those who
have gone through
the same to take
a stand.

Patterns Of Your Touch|

Smear your thumbprints
in swirls over all that you
find alluring– let them be
smudged with your flaws.
Make them your own and
design your imperfections;
they are alluring as well.
        They deserve your affection.

Too Human For Earth|

Here is something I hold deep: I daydream, often, of places far and far away. I imagine myself in the warm Arizona weather, the Grand Canyon reflecting itself back at me with its bright red-orange tint from the photos I've seen. The sun dipping into the panorama, and I, with my arms outstretched above my head; a widened smile plastered on my face and the warmth of the wind blowing my hair everywhere. I am free. I visualize myself leaving a piece of my heart there and taking a part of the breathtaking view with me in return; an exchange.

I imagine myself in front of the Las Vegas lights: women, men, and jazzy blues making their way through my eardrums... they are everywhere and they invite me in. It is a swarm of endless dancing and laughter. Humans being humans, enjoying life in a place that they can escape the reality of their lives. I join them because I yearn this; the liberation, the escape, the innocent carelessness. It doesn't matter, so long as I live to see tomorrow.

I envision myself in a mass array of places, capturing every moment in mental stills, leaving pieces of me everywhere in exchange for a memory. I wouldn't regret it, I wouldn't one single bit, if tomorrow came and all that was left of me were fragments of the places I'd seen. I'd be free.

Millennials|

The heat of our euphoria was an addiction—
we refused to belong to anyone;
when internally, we belonged
                    to everybody.
Externally, we portrayed a version
of ourselves that conveyed
an unreachable utopia.
                    Edited photos,
edited conversations,
edited connections.
We snipped and
                    slit away
at our uniqueness until
we were left with
blank pages of
                    sameness.

Natural Disasters|

Surround yourself with
people that will lift
you when gravity
works overtime.

At some point,
it will.

The mental volcano will erupt
and its molten lava
will descend upon
you.

Some problems only dissolve
with proper guidance.

Youth |

Let the thrill be your mentor.
It doesn't have to be dangerous.
Find them in the sacred small places
                                    of your life—

midnights on the beach,
open sunroof summers,
the guy you hit it off
with at the carnival.

                        Live your youth

don't let it
outlive
you.

Carousel|

It is a motion sickness;
building slowly, repeatedly, agonizingly.

You will rotate like a carousel,
dizziness and confusion will overtake you.

There will be fear. There will be excitement.
If he is good to you, it will be worth it.

Peace Did Not Come Easy|

"How does it feel to be a seamlessly ethereal being?"

I was walking on clouds, his grip was light on my elbow, as if he was aware that I could float away at any given moment.

"It is like all that I've been working toward, since I could speak, has finally been accomplished."

Manipulation|

If you find your legs spreading wide
while your self-esteem is sinking low,
closely look at the person that you are giving
your most intimate self to.
Some will wrap themselves around you
and others will throw themselves on you.

You Will Be Stronger After|

The only source of pain that I've known
is the kind that empties your gut–
the type that gradually inflates
it with air instead.

It bloats to the size of a blimp
pleading for acknowledgment
by the very person it was intended for.

It has called my attention far too often;
far too often, I have disregarded
the muffles of long lost
hurt.

If you are like me, opt to bear it.
Deprive it from resurfacing
out of the unknown.

The Other Side|

What we often see ahead is a milky white fence, as if it were freshly coated that very morning, one could faintly smell the sour paint lingering. We see clear cut grass, with flowers of every variety blooming in its own patch of land. A plethora of fruits and vegetables overwhelm a lime-green garden; tomatoes, carrots, potatoes of every kind. Apples sprout from the perked trees eager for a gust to knock them down to liberty– free from the grips of its branches. We see abundance in front of us, so very close, yet we are barricaded behind this tall beautifully designed fence. We selfishly want it for ourselves– how can it be so easy?

What we don't often see are the weeds that sprout overnight or the hands that exchange beauty and softness for the sake of another life, for the sake of creation– what are we living for if we are not sacrificing for the sake of creation? Our eyes dismiss the pulsing veins that work to pull soil apart like the red sea so that food can come to fruition. It is not until you keenly observe that you witness the exhausted individual, on the other side of the fence, on his knees, so that he too, could see the same white picket fence as you.

Healing My Skin|

"How can you continue living, like normal, with all those cracks beneath your skin?"

You softly grazed your fingers along my hips as we lay side by side, our backs to the brown soil, among a field of sunflowers. The big blue cloaked itself above us, clouds tenderly floated across to another part of town.

"They are a part of me, just like you are a part of me. The cracks are the paths and you were the destination."

The Lady In Red|

As the globe continued to spin
a whirl of black and white,
to him, she was the
slight bit of color.

The Rest Will Follow|

Do you want to know how to succeed?
Let all that you do burn with passion;
set it ablaze, haphazardly,
without any worry as to
who is watching.

Display it on large billboards,
lights coddling them– where
you are the maker
and the admirer.
          Do it all but do it with conviction.

A Voice Within|

The streets sat silent and still,
no one lingered on the deserted paths.
The alleyways, dressed in graffiti,
       stole the show.
I had strolled the sidewalks
looking for nothing in particular,
when a voice whispered,
"Take note of the nuisances in life–
they often lead you where you're meant to be."

My Feet Aren't Tired Yet|

I have been confused for twenty-three years but of one thing I am certain; I will climb the steepest hills and let the brisk gusts prick me like individual ice picks. They will not intimidate me because the obstacles I've fought to overcome, came and went. By the grace of all things on our land, I prevailed. The cracks beneath me prove it.

Poker|

There is nothing more self-destructive
than being afraid of your own potential.

It makes you forget that there are
far more options than aces.

Darling, you are a wild card—
you were destined to play any hand.

Earth Mother|

Herbs are nature's gift to health.
I hope that I can heal the
planet as much as
it has worked
to heal us.

Perfection Is Man-made|

The earth does not revolve in a perfect circle,
she is chiseled by the pain she's faced—
every tremble, shake, and quake.

She has exuded beauty since
the birth of time and space.

Not once has she measured
the outer value of her tribulations.
Why should you?

She Holds Her Power|

Once she decided to coexist with the magic from within, she ceased to be the same since then.

From Here To Where? |

"Think about it, we can leave today, anywhere we want in the world. We can hop on an airplane right now, we can start all over again. We could explore the fields that you've always envisioned, hop on one of the canoes and migrate west with the swans. It doesn't have to be this way forever. Everything can change."

The notion was an idealization of all she had pleaded from him; here he was, using them as a gesture for her to stay. She wanted to ask him if it was real, this newly paved two-way street. A prospect of a new beginning. A response spilled out from her lips before she could swallow them back, she had withdrawn them as a habit previously. This time, the words came thick from her mouth but still, she replied drearily,

"The question is, will you? Will we?"

Juggler|

Nightmares began when
he handed you over
the rights to his doubts and
a compilation of hidden
insecurities
        to care for.

He didn't inform you that
they would swell to the size
of grapefruits until your spine
slumped into a
        crescent moon.

I am here to tell you,
it is not your fault.
You aren't his performance
        and you are your own art.

Mold and Grime|

Do not let anyone rot your vivaciousness.
They can't comprehend what it's like to
have a forest growing in your chest—
when they've spent cycles
          not tending to their own.

No Limitations|

She lived writing in the same way that she inhaled
her oxygen; steadily and without restriction.
Fluorescent lights lined her ceiling, pages upon
pages dispersed around her– a forcefield made up
of her work. A shield of protection. It would bloat
to such a size that humanity would have no choice
but to breathe her words as she does.

Simple Gestures|

"You know, it's funny, how one person can assume that they've got it all set. Then, one day, someone else comes along and makes you question every detail of your life. You did that. I need you to know... you make me want to do more than everything I have ever accomplished."

Two children moved about a couple of feet away from us, building sandcastles with plastic buckets. One little girl wore her hair in two pigtails, she was cautiously placing an assortment of decorative flags around the crown of the castle. The other child, a young boy, was using his blue toy pickup truck to haul sand over. Out of my peripheral vision, I would periodically see him find a crab, delicately grab it and place it back into the ocean. I observed with concealed admiration at the ingenuous purity in the act.

Gently wrapping an arm around your waist, I responded, *"for me, you've done more than you can possibly know."*

Gems|

Cherish our children;
their tiny frames
hold answers.

They will teach us like we did them—
our muscles no longer able to transmit
the information that they can.

Take care of them.
They are our hidden gems.

Lessons |

In some parts of the world, cold weather only lasts a season. When you're down on your luck remember that summer is right around the corner. All you have to do is walk.

Life should be lived as if there were only one chance at every opportunity, very few are lucky to receive a second or a third. Why complicate them with a one-dimensional emotion like fear?

Among a colossal group of 'Nos' there is always bound to be one yes. Always ask the question, the answer gets you on the path that you're destined.

People aren't glue and that's okay. Some stick and some slip; enjoy their company despite the fact. Love again– it's all we're left with when all else seems distant.

Silhouette|

"Show me something beautiful."
He switched off the lights–
she stood; a gleaming figure.
"Beauty is what shines in
the darkest of spaces.
I'm lucky to say, I believe
I've found my favorite
silhouette."

You Are Patient, I Am Kind|

Take me slow.
We don't have to know
where we're meant to go.

I just want our deserved title;
the sweet and tender,
soft and supple.

Dear, dear love.
Please be good to me.
I have searched so long for you

and you,
have waited
so long for we.

Noise |

She cupped his cheeks between her hands,
pulled him close to her and said,
"in a world drowned in noise,
we often forget to look at each other."
The sound of traffic dimmed behind them,
they forgot about the crying children

and the screeching sound of an impatient city.
All at once, he realized she was right.
He had never looked into her eyes before.
A flicker of want reflected back to him.
And he knew, if she asked,
he'd never speak again.

Codes|

You are discreetly etched into the pages of my book
and I hope you realize, in due time,
that the good ones—the poems—
are spilled verses written
in your name.

Relationship Formula|

The distance
between two hearts is the sum
of here and however far each other
is willing to travel;
dividing the responsibilities
in half so that the circumference
doesn't stretch too wide.
They say the distance of
a mile can't be found
on a negative plane
but maybe the deeper
that you explore into
each other, the further you'll go.
You can go everywhere.
The negatives can turn to positives
if only you find their absolute values.
Turn it into something more.
Explore the possibilities.
When it is a real number
there is only one right answer.
Solve for why, when you are uncertain,
no matter how complex
the equation gets.

Trinkets|

My feet will cover oceans—
my neck adorned in shells.
I will be my own until the
day that I am whole.

My pockets will
bulge with memories—
a collection I will treasure
to share with you
       the day that you are whole too.

Photographs|

I want to remember these mementos
of when I ached to have more;
I had abundance all around me.

When money becomes principal,
I want to remember that it is not
what I will be nostalgic for.

I will mourn my best days
because even though I didn't have much,
it was all that I needed. It was enough.

Dignity|

You may have lost in abundance
but what you have gained
within yourself is worth
much more.

Separate We Rise, Together We Fall|

We are like snowflakes—
each individually different,
still and all, we melt the same.

Batter Up!|

He will come again
with a recharged battery
and he will try to bat you down.

Three strikes and he's out.

You did not get a home run
when he stood on
your field.

Reclaim your power.

If not, he will always believe
that you revel in the
losing team.

Help Build Podiums|

Never attempt to
dismantle another
person's confidence.

It may be their
pedestal when
there is nowhere
          else for them to stand on.

Living in Limbo|

I can't help but to
silently commend those
that presume they can't but do anyway.
It is standard to be barred by others
but condemning oneself is
a grave dug early.

Sunrise|

"If you could fly anywhere, right now,
where would your wings take you?"
        "Wherever the sun is rising."
He slightly angled his chin and pondered,
"why is that?"
        "It reminds me I can dream another day."

Disarray|

I used to organize my books—
tallest to smallest,
thickest to thinnest.

My hangers—
color coded; my jeans,
lightest to darkest.

When spring came,
I donated the excess
and got rid of the rest.

I met you when summer crept.
You told me flowers grew wild;
among them I slept.

You made me proud
to grow a life
unafraid of disarray.

If it meant living chronologically
with you and me—
from night to(day).

A Story Not Yet Told|

When we met: we agreed that we would do everything in halves. I made the coffee, you watched the morning news in nothing but briefs and the scent of men's aftershave, taking a pull from your smoke. Once the coffee was ready, you would take your mug and mine; set them both on the marble white counter, carefully grab the carafe by its handle, and serve into our mugs as the sound of warm coffee being poured reverberated around the room.

On our first official date: I wore silk and a pair of heels; you didn't try to outdo me because you wanted me to be the light in the room, however, you made me laugh and offered to pay the tab. I was the light in the room but your light was shared with me and no one else. I would do anything to nourish it.

When we first met: You gave me a slight smile, as if you had already known that this was it. Truth be told, none of us really knew at the time and it seemed as though the more we attempted to seek equilibrium in other people– we lost it for ourselves. We waited. It would come to be five years before we synced our flow.

When we met: I knew it would be worth the wait.

Muse|

You're my mosaic, my abstract, my layers,
my darling–
the ripples, the shadows, a portrait,
my landscape.

You're a watercolor sky
among clear distinct mountains.
What kind of artist am I,
if not defined by my canvas?

Proverbs|

I have yet to come across a passage
that, in its wisdom, will convince me
of a more succumbing life, a life outside of here,
     where the grass remains wet in its excitement
and our luminous sky is better than clear. Reflected
at its surface– a sky beaded in stars yet seen.
     None of that could come close in its purpose,
in comparison of what being with you
has made my life to mean.

Thank You|

How can you tell me that brown is poor?
When I am so rich

                    with love?

It taught me all that I know—
left me branded with mild
emblems of reassurance.

        I am all that I am because
        brown has always been

                    generous.

Handle With Care|

Never accustom yourself to counting bruises,
they should only serve as reminders
to never carry someone else's
burdens as your own.

His Letter|

He used to watch her climb trees— how she would press her sneaker on the stumps of the trunk and prop herself up using its branches. *"Why do you enjoy climbing so much?"* he would always ask her. She would respond with a laugh and proceed to shuffle the leafiest branch so that they would scatter down on him. *"You get a great view of what you have when you see it from a larger perspective."*

From below, while you explored, I explored you in every form. The crease in your white sneakers birthed from endless summers of climbing. The way you bent and twisted to find the best view–testing branches for durability. How when I called up to you, you laughed and shook leaves so that they would shower above me. Though it's been a year, I could still sense the adrenaline you felt–being so far up. Peaceful and yet exhilarating. I could imagine because that's what I felt with you. From our years of us together, I could say, 'you were the only scene worth viewing.' Wherever you are I hope it's in the form of an apple orchard. That way when I see one, I'll never forget our springs and how they kept us infinite.

Albums|

Her recollections were somewhere
in the nectar of their linear love.
They were gone.
The familiar intimacy she extended to him,
their table of events had reached their end;
it was all or nothing.
Fables were written in their wrinkles;
horseback rides in the urban wilderness,
rope swings into the water.
Johnny Cash playing– a blaring Pontiac firebird.
This was a thing called love;
but why? If today, it had
become lost on her.
"You are in the albums that we forged,
I may have failed to remember them all but
without them I'd be nothing."

Tranquility's Flow|

The river brought my essence peace.
She dyed her womb with the pebbles
that were brave enough to
survive the stream.

She cascaded down the slopes,
flowed as if it were done
specifically for me.

The idea may be obscene but
I am soothed by her scene.

Brothers And Sisters|

Learn the world,
analyze the spaces
that most excite your
                 curiosity.
Become versed in its form
from every angle.
                 Then, teach another.

Women's Empowerment|

We hold the weight of our breasts
in the breadth of our limbs.
It is more than nutrients
            and vitamins.
Generations before ours were
replenished from our alleged
unveiled shameless
            sins.
We constructed knights
with naturally forged
equipment
            and we're blamed for it.

History|

You are a lioness;
your hair is boisterous,
animated, vibrant.

    Do not explain it.
Your posture stands stern;
the tales of your parents' parents
hold you up on a wooden totem pole.

    Do not explain it.
Marvel at your inner kingdom;
it is something they will
fight to comprehend

    but do not explain it.
Your culture does not
need their biased
justification.

You Before Them|

Be the Goddess that you wore born to be.
Drape yourself in fine satin;
recapture it for future
reference.

Enjoy your own recognition before
devoting your unforgiving
seconds to unforgiving
people.

A Moment|

A moment of silence
for the youth that loved
and lost their lives
to mindless
minds.

Humans can be so defected that they will gamble
on another person's life because of their own
inner demons. We, individually, have gone
through our own tribulations but some were
deprived of the opportunities to grow as people
with no good reason.

A page. Dedicated to them. Write their names in.

Do It All Again|

Hold on to your truth,
it will be your wakeup call;
there may have been many ends
and because of them, there
have also been numerous
beginnings.

A LETTER TO THE SURVIVORS

It does not matter how big or how small, you have
survived it all. No one can define for you how hard
it is to get up in the morning. No one can tell you
how bad your chest hurts after losing a loved one.
No one can force upon you feelings. All we could
do is try and support one another. Every day, we
wake up, tie our shoelaces; we walk. You've made
it. The oxygen– it circulates inside of you with
every breath. We've all made it. You've survived
that morning rush hour, that unreasonable
coworker, that tough breakup, you survived college
or high school (or both), you survived his death
grip, his unwanted touch. You gave love a hug; you
went in and loved again. You reclaimed your heart.
It is so difficult I know. But I commend you, if no
one congratulates you for waking up today, then, I
will. You woke up today, you gave someone
meaning with your presence. Thank You.

ABOUT THE BOOK

'The Cracks Beneath Me' began as an outlet for a traumatic experience that I went through at the end of spring of 2017. It was essentially a poetic journal for my thoughts and emotions when I was trying to make sense of what had happened to me. Over time, it started to evolve into a book and I decided to, well, run with it. As the collection grew, I became immersed in the process of spreading my message. The message being, overcoming toxic, overbearing, and abusive relationships. Like any human being, I bounced back and forth– should I open myself up to another person again? Will I ever be able to regain the bit of confidence I ever had? Is walking out the door and facing sunlight again even worth it? The truth of the matter is that, to me, it most certainly is. However, throughout the collection you will see that the confusion of the human condition is apparent. I dissolve myself into fantasies and realities of wanting to be with someone after being abused but then taking all of my words back. I go back and forth trying to figure these things out but, in the end, we're not meant to know all the answers. Confusion is normal. All we can do is continue to grow and be the best we can be because being a person didn't come with a rulebook, a set of guidelines, or even a description.

ABOUT THE AUTHOR

Idelis Llenas, a fellow writer and lover of creative expression, grew up in The Bronx, New York. The struggles of growing up in a low-income family motivated her to delve into writing at a very young age. As a child, she was the top reader and writer in her class. Her love for writing has, since then, followed her into adulthood. When she isn't writing, she is studying for school, eating sushi, spending time with her family, and binging on her favorite shows (The Office, How I Met Your Mother). This is her first poetry collection out of, hopefully, many more to come.